THE NATURE OF JESUS

When Jesus was Born, did He inherit a sinful nature?

Dr. Maxwell Shimba

Shimba Publishing, LLC.

TABLE OF CONTENTS

INTRODUCTION

The essence of Christ's nature, both human and divine, has long captivated theologians, scholars, and believers worldwide. This dual nature poses profound questions about the intersection of divinity with humanity, especially concerning the concept of sin. The purpose of this book is to explore these complex theological questions and present a detailed examination of Jesus Christ as both fully human and fully divine. Through this exploration, the book aims to provide readers with a clearer understanding of key Christian doctrines and their implications for faith and practice.

The inquiry into whether Jesus, being both divine and human, inherited a sinful nature is particularly significant. This question not only probes the depths of Christological doctrines but also touches on issues of salvation, atonement, and human nature itself. By addressing these topics, the book seeks to enrich the reader's theological knowledge and deepen their spiritual insights.

Overview of the Theological Questions Regarding Jesus Christ's Nature and Sin

At the heart of Christian theology lies a paradox: Jesus Christ is professed to be both fully God and fully man. This foundational belief prompts several questions that are vital to both academic theology and personal faith. How can Jesus be both divine and human? If He was human, did He inherit the sinful nature that, according to scripture, affects all humans? If He did not, what does that say about His humanity? How does His nature affect our understanding of sin, redemption, and the human condition?

These questions are not merely academic; they have profound implications for Christian belief and practice. They influence our understanding of doctrines such as the Incarnation, the Atonement, and the character of God. They also impact how believers live out their faith in concepts such as sin, grace, and redemption.

This book will delve into these issues by examining biblical texts, historical theological perspectives, and contemporary scholarly discussions. It will explore different viewpoints within the Christian tradition, providing a balanced view that respects the diversity of thought that has historically surrounded this topic.

Through this exploration, "The Nature of Christ: Humanity, Divinity, and Sin" aims to provide a comprehensive guide to one of the most profound and beautiful mysteries of the Christian faith—the nature of Jesus Christ. This introduction sets the stage for a deeper dive into the dual nature of Christ, inviting readers on a journey that promises not only to inform but also to transform.

DR. MAXWELL SHIMBA

CHAPTER 01

THE INCARNATION OF CHRIST

The doctrine of the Incarnation is a cornerstone of Christian theology. It proclaims that Jesus Christ, the second person of the Holy Trinity, took on human flesh. This event transcends mere appearance or illusion; it asserts that God truly became man while remaining fully divine. The Gospel of John encapsulates this mystery succinctly: "And the Word became flesh and dwelt among us" (John 1:14). This statement is not merely symbolic but literal—asserting that God entered into the human condition in a real and tangible way.

The concept of Incarnation is rooted deeply in the scriptures. Old Testament prophecies, such as Isaiah 7:14 ("Behold, the virgin shall conceive and bear a son, and shall call his name Immanuel") and Isaiah 9:6 ("For to us a child is born, to us a son is given"), set the stage for the coming of a divine figure in human form. These prophecies are fulfilled in the New Testament, as seen in the narratives of Christ's birth in the Gospels of Matthew and Luke. These accounts detail the miraculous nature of Jesus' birth, affirming His divine origin and human presence.

The Incarnation is pivotal for several reasons. Firstly, it demonstrates God's profound love and commitment to His creation. By becoming human, God the Son chose to experience the fullness of human life, including its limitations and sufferings, except sin. This act underscores God's empathy and solidarity with humanity.

Secondly, the Incarnation is essential for salvation. According to Christian theology, only a being who is both God and man can mediate between humanity and God, offering a sacrifice sufficient to atone for the sins of the world. Thus, Jesus' dual nature is not an arcane doctrinal point but a vital truth that relates to the salvation of all humanity.

Christ's Humanity and Divinity

In exploring Christ's humanity, the Gospels provide numerous instances of Jesus experiencing human emotions and physical needs—He felt hunger (Matthew 4:2), wept (John 11:35), and showed compassion (Matthew 9:36). Yet, alongside these human traits, Jesus also exhibited divine attributes; He performed miracles, forgave sins, and declared eternal truths about God's kingdom.

The mystery of the Incarnation lies in this perfect and simultaneous expression of both natures. The Council of Chalcedon (451 AD) articulated this understanding in a formal statement, declaring that Jesus is to be acknowledged in two natures, without confusion, without change, without division, without separation—the distinction of the natures being by no means taken away by the union, but rather the characteristics of each nature being preserved.

Contemporary Reflections on the Incarnation

In contemporary theology, the Incarnation is discussed not only in light of scriptural and historical doctrines but also regarding its implications for modern Christian life and ethics. It challenges believers to reflect on God's accessibility and vulnerability, inviting a response of awe, worship, and imitation. It encourages Christians to engage in acts of humility, service, and compassion, following the example of Christ, who, though divine, did not disdain the lowliness of human experience.

Thus, the doctrine of the Incarnation stands as a profound testament to God's love and commitment to His creation. It affirms that in Jesus Christ, heaven and earth meet, divinity and humanity converge, and the story of redemption is intimately woven into the fabric of human history. This chapter sets the foundation for understanding how this profound truth impacts the discussions on the nature of sin and the sinlessness of Jesus, explored in the subsequent chapters.

BIBLICAL REFERENCES TO JESUS AS FULLY HUMAN AND FULLY DIVINE

The Christian faith is fundamentally centered on the belief in Jesus Christ as both fully human and fully divine. This dual nature is crucial for understanding His role in salvation history. This chapter explores the various biblical texts that underscore both aspects of Christ's nature, providing a scriptural foundation for this central doctrine.

Jesus a Fully Human

The humanity of Jesus is well-documented throughout the New Testament. The Gospels portray His human experiences vividly:

1. Birth and Lineage: The narratives of Jesus' birth in Matthew 1:18-25 and Luke 2:1-7 emphasize His human origin, detailing His birth to Mary, a virgin, in Bethlehem. Genealogies in Matthew 1 and Luke 3 trace His lineage back to David and Abraham, underscoring His membership in the human family.

2. Physical and Emotional Experiences: Jesus experienced hunger (Matthew 4:2), thirst (John 19:28), and

fatigue (John 4:6). He displayed emotions such as joy (Luke 10:21), sorrow (John 11:35), and anger (Mark 3:5). These instances affirm His full participation in the human condition.

3. Temptation: In Matthew 4:1-11, Jesus is tempted by Satan in the wilderness. This episode highlights His human vulnerability to temptation, though He remains sinless, responding with scripture to repel each temptation.

Jesus as Fully Divine

Conversely, the New Testament is replete with references to Jesus' divinity, illustrating His nature as God incarnate:

1. Pre-existence: John 1:1-14 declares Jesus as the Word who was with God in the beginning and who was God. This pre-existence indicates His divine nature and active role in creation.

2. Miracles: Jesus performed numerous miracles—calming storms (Mark 4:35-41), multiplying loaves and fish (John 6:5-14), healing the sick (Matthew 8:14-17), and raising the dead (John 11:43-44). These acts demonstrate His command over nature, illness, and death, reflecting divine power.

3. Forgiveness of Sins: In several passages (e.g., Mark 2:5-12), Jesus forgives sins, an act attributed only to God. His ability to forgive sins underscores His divine authority.

4. Transfiguration: The Transfiguration (Matthew 17:1-9) presents Jesus in divine glory, witnessed by Peter, James, and John, who see Him conversing with Moses and Elijah. This event manifests His divine nature alongside His humanity.

5. Resurrection and Ascension: The resurrection (Luke 24:1-53) and ascension (Acts 1:9-11) of Jesus are pivotal events that affirm His divinity. Overcoming death and ascending into heaven are portrayed as divine acts, marking His authority over life and death.

Theological Synthesis

The doctrine of the Hypostatic Union, as articulated by the Council of Chalcedon, affirms that Jesus Christ is recognized in two natures, fully God and fully man, united in one person without mixture or confusion. This theological position is supported by the scriptural references laid out above, which together provide a comprehensive picture of a being who bridges heaven and earth, embodying both the divine and the human.

The biblical portrayal of Jesus as both fully human and fully divine is not merely a doctrinal point but is central to the Christian understanding of salvation. His humanity allows Him to identify with us, suffering as we do, yet without sin. His divinity ensures that His sacrifice is sufficient for the atonement of sins for all humanity. Thus, these scriptural insights form the bedrock of faith, inviting believers to trust in the profound mystery and grace of the Incarnation. This foundation is essential for exploring further theological implications, such as the nature of Christ's sinlessness and His role in redemption, discussed in subsequent chapters.

HISTORICAL PERSPECTIVE ON THE INCARNATION

The doctrine of the Incarnation, which posits that Jesus Christ is both fully divine and fully human, has been a focal point of Christian theology since the earliest days of the faith. This chapter explores how various historical periods and thinkers have interpreted and understood this central Christian doctrine, highlighting the development and challenges it has faced over the centuries.

The first few centuries of the Christian Church were marked by vigorous debates as early church fathers sought to clarify and define the nature of Christ's Incarnation. These discussions were crucial in shaping orthodox Christian beliefs.

1. Apostolic Fathers and Apologists: Early Christian writers like Ignatius of Antioch and Justin Martyr emphasized the reality of Jesus' humanity and divinity, defending against contemporary heresies that denied one nature or the other.

2. The Arian Controversy: Arius, a fourth-century priest, argued that Jesus, while supernatural, was not co-eternal with the Father and thus not truly divine. This controversy led to the First Council of Nicaea in 325 AD, which rejected Arianism and affirmed the full divinity of Christ, as expressed in the Nicene Creed.

3. The Council of Chalcedon: Perhaps the most definitive statement on the Incarnation came in 451 AD with the Council of Chalcedon. The Chalcedonian Definition declared that Jesus is to be recognized in two natures, fully God and fully man, united in one person "without confusion, without change, without division, without separation."

Medieval Theologians and Mystics

During the medieval period, theologians and mystics further explored the implications of the Incarnation, often focusing on its mystical and existential dimensions.

1. Anselm of Canterbury: In his work Cur Deus Homo ("Why God Became Man"), Anselm argued that only a being who was both God and man could achieve the redemption of humanity, thus providing a rational basis for the necessity of the Incarnation.

2. Thomas Aquinas: Aquinas provided a detailed systematic theology concerning Christ's nature in his Summa Theologica. He discussed the unity of Christ's human and

divine wills and how His human nature was assumed but not absorbed by His divine nature.

3. Mystical Perspectives: Mystics like Julian of Norwich and Hildegard of Bingen reflected on the Incarnation in deeply personal terms, seeing in it the expression of God's boundless love for humanity and the intimate connection between the divine and the human.

The Reformation and Modern Era

The Protestant Reformation and the subsequent development of modern Christian thought brought new perspectives and reaffirmations concerning the Incarnation.

1. Reformers: Figures like Martin Luther and John Calvin emphasized the importance of Christ's humanity and divinity for understanding His atoning work on the cross. They argued that both natures were crucial for the legal and relational aspects of salvation.

2. Liberal Theology: In the modern era, some theologians began to question traditional doctrines about the Incarnation, often focusing on the moral and ethical teachings of Jesus rather than His divine nature. However, conservative and orthodox theologians have continually reaffirmed the traditional understanding of the Incarnation as essential to Christian faith.

3.   Ecumenical Dialogues: Recent theological discussions have often occurred in an ecumenical context, with various Christian denominations exploring and sometimes resolving long-standing differences over Christological doctrines, emphasizing a shared commitment to the mystery of the Incarnation.

Throughout history, the doctrine of the Incarnation has been central to Christian theological reflection and has been interpreted in various ways depending on cultural, philosophical, and theological contexts. Each period has contributed layers of understanding to this profound doctrine, reflecting the ongoing attempt to comprehend the unfathomable mystery of God-made flesh. This historical journey not only enriches our theological heritage but also challenges contemporary believers to continually seek a deeper understanding of the significance of the Incarnation for faith and practice today.

THE PRE-EXISTENCE OF CHRIST: CONFESSIONS AND APOSTOLIC TESTIMONIES

The doctrine of the pre-existence of Jesus Christ posits that He existed before His incarnation and human birth. This chapter delves into biblical affirmations of this doctrine, examining the confessions of Jesus Himself and the apostolic testimonies about His divine origin, utilizing the King James Version (KJV) of the Bible and supporting exegesis for a deeper understanding.

Jesus' Own Confessions of Pre-Existence

1. John 8:58 - Jesus said, "Verily, verily, I say unto you, Before Abraham was, I am." This statement links Jesus to the divine name revealed to Moses in Exodus 3:14, "I AM THAT I AM," asserting His eternal nature and identity with God.

Expository Commentary: In this passage, Jesus not only claims existence before Abraham, a foundational patriarch but also uses the term "I am," which in the Hebrew context is directly connected to Yahweh, the self-existent One. This declaration was understood by His contemporaries as a claim to divinity, as evidenced by their subsequent attempt to stone Him for blasphemy.

2. John 17:5 - In His high priestly prayer, Jesus asks, "And now, O Father, glorify thou me with thine own self with the glory which I had with thee before the world was."

Expository Commentary: Here, Jesus speaks of a shared glory with the Father prior to the creation of the world, indicating His active participation in the eternal realm before His incarnation. This speaks to the inter-trinitarian relationship and the eternal divine fellowship.

Apostolic Confessions of Christ's Divinity and Pre-Existence

1. John 1:1-3 - "In the beginning was the Word, and the Word was with God, and the Word was God. The same was true in the beginning with God. All things were made by him; and without him was not anything made that was made."

Expository Commentary: The Apostle John opens his Gospel with a profound declaration of Jesus' divine nature and pre-existence. The term "Word" (Logos) signifies Jesus' pre-incarnate existence and His role in creation, affirming His deity and eternal presence with God.

2. Colossians 1:16-17 - "For by him were all things created, that are in heaven, and that are in earth, visible and invisible, whether they be thrones, or dominions, or principalities, or powers: all things were created by him, and for him: And he is before all things, and by him, all things consist."

Expository Commentary: Paul emphasizes Jesus' pre-eminent role in creation, affirming that not only were all things made through Him and for Him, but He also existed before all things, further underscoring His pre-existence and sustaining power over the universe.

3. Philippians 2:6-7 - "Who, being in the form of God, thought it not robbery to be equal with God: But made

himself of no reputation, and took upon him the form of a servant, and was made in the likeness of men."

Expository Commentary: This passage reflects on Jesus' pre-incarnate state where He existed in the "form of God" and chose to humble Himself to become human. The phrase "thought it not robbery to be equal with God" indicates that Jesus' equality with God was not something grasped or usurped but inherently His.

The doctrine of Christ's pre-existence is foundational to understanding His divine nature and mission. Biblical testimonies from Jesus Himself and His earliest followers provide clear and profound evidence of His existence before the world began, underscoring His role as the Creator and Sustainer. These scriptural insights not only affirm the deity of Christ but also enhance our understanding of the Incarnation, as they depict a Savior who originates in eternity and enters time, bridging the infinite and the finite. This chapter lays a vital foundation for comprehending the full scope of Jesus' identity and work as depicted in Scripture.

UNDERSTANDING EHYEH ASHER EHYEH: THE DEPTH OF DIVINE SELF- SELF-IDENTIFICATION

The phrase 'Ehyeh Asher Ehyeh' (אֶהְיֶה אֲשֶׁר אֶהְיֶה), found in Exodus 3:14, represents one of the most profound self-disclosures of God in the Hebrew Scriptures. Translated variously as "I am who I am," "I will be what I will be," and other similar renditions, this declaration offers deep insights into the nature of God. This chapter explores the different facets of this phrase, examining its theological significance, implications, and echo in the New Testament.

Etymological Exploration

'Ehyeh' is the first-person singular imperfect form of the verb "to be" (hayah) in Hebrew. The imperfect tense in Hebrew often expresses ongoing, uncompleted action, which in this context can imply timelessness or eternal existence. The repetition of 'Ehyeh' with 'Asher' (which means "who," "what," or "that") intensifies the focus on the subject—God Himself—emphasizing His self-existence and self-sufficiency.

Theological Implications

1. Self-Existence and Eternality: The phrase "I am who I am" underscores God's independence from all things. Unlike humans and all created beings who define themselves

through relationships or activities, God's existence is underived and self-sustained. This self-definition points to God's aseity—an attribute describing His self-existence without origin.

2. Immutability: "I will be what I will be" suggests God's unchanging nature. What He is, He always has been and always will be. This immutability reassures that His character, promises, and purposes are steadfast and reliable over time.

3. Mystery and Incomprehensibility: The phrase can also be seen as an expression of divine mystery. By essentially saying He is who He is, God indicates that the fullness of His nature is beyond human comprehension. This declaration invites reverence and awe, acknowledging the limits of human understanding.

4. Dynamic Presence in History: The alternative translation, "I will become what I choose to become," or "I create what(ever) I create," speaks to God's active, dynamic presence in history. It suggests that God is not static but continually works out His will in the unfolding of time, emphasizing His role as Creator and Sustainer.

Scriptural Context

The context of Exodus 3:14 is pivotal—God speaks this phrase to Moses at the burning bush when commissioning him to lead the Israelites out of Egypt. Here, God's self-identification is linked to His covenant faithfulness and redemptive action. This declaration assures Moses—and Israel—that the God who promises deliverance is eternally present and capable of fulfilling His promises.

New Testament Echoes

The phrase resonates in the New Testament through the words of Jesus, particularly in the Gospel of John. Jesus' repeated use of "I am" (Greek: ego eimi) statements (e.g., John 8:58, "Before Abraham was, I am") directly connects to 'Ehyeh, linking His identity with the God of Exodus. This linguistic and conceptual connection serves to assert Jesus' divinity and His role in the divine plan of salvation, bridging the covenant promises of the Old Testament with their fulfillment in the New.

'Ehyeh Asher Ehyeh' is not just a cryptic puzzle left for theologians to decipher but a profound revelation of God's nature and His interaction with the world. This declaration encompasses God's eternity, immutability, mysteriousness, and active presence in human history, all of which anchor the biblical narrative and Christian faith. By exploring this phrase, believers gain not only a deeper understanding of who God is but also a greater appreciation for His works and His ways throughout Scripture and history.

This foundational concept thus serves as a bridge connecting God's eternal nature with His loving, ongoing engagement with His creation.

CHAPTER 02

THE HUMANITY OF JESUS CHRIST

In Christian theology, the humanity of Jesus Christ is as crucial as His divinity. It is through His human nature that Jesus fully participates in the human experience, allowing Him to be the perfect mediator between God and humanity. This chapter explores the various aspects of Jesus' humanity, demonstrating that He was indeed 100% human, a fundamental truth that has profound theological and practical implications for believers.

Biblical Evidence of Jesus' Humanity

1. Birth and Growth: The Gospels begin the story of Jesus with His birth to Mary in Bethlehem (Luke 2:4-7). He grew up in a family, had brothers and sisters (Mark 6:3), and grew in wisdom and stature (Luke 2:52). These elements of birth, family life, and development are intrinsic to human experience.

2. Physical Needs and Emotions: Jesus experienced hunger (Matthew 4:2), thirst (John 19:28), and fatigue (John 4:6). He displayed a range of emotions including joy (Luke 10:21), anger (Mark 3:5), compassion (Matthew 9:36), and profound sorrow (John 11:35). These responses are characteristic of the human condition.

3. Temptations: The temptation of Jesus in the wilderness (Matthew 4:1-11) is a significant testament to His humanity. He was tempted in all ways as we are, yet without sin (Hebrews 4:15). This aspect of Jesus' life not only underscores His humanity but also His moral triumph as a human.

4. Social Interactions and Relationships: Jesus had close friendships, as seen in His relationships with Mary, Martha, and Lazarus (John 11:5), and He felt betrayed (Matthew 26:20-25). His interactions with His disciples show Him teaching, rebuking, and caring for them, further highlighting His engagement in human social dynamics.

Theological Significance of Jesus' Humanity

1. Relatability: Jesus' human experiences make Him relatable to us in every way. This relatability is crucial for His role as a mediator (1 Timothy 2:5). Because He has experienced human life firsthand, He understands our struggles, joys, and pains.

2. Redemptive Role: As a sinless human, Jesus' death on the cross has redemptive value for humanity. His humanity is essential for the atoning sacrifice, as only a human could pay the penalty for human sins, and only a sinless human could do so effectively (Hebrews 2:17).

3. Model of Holiness: In His human life, Jesus serves as a model of holiness and obedience to God (1 Peter 2:21-24). His life provides a tangible example of how to live in accordance with God's will, despite the challenges inherent in human nature.

Historical and Creedal Affirmations

The early church vigorously defended the reality of Jesus' humanity against Docetism, a heresy that claimed Jesus only seemed to be human. The Chalcedonian Creed (451 AD) robustly affirms that Jesus is "truly man" and made "like us in all respects, apart from sin." These historical declarations are critical in underscoring the orthodox Christian belief in Jesus' full humanity.

Practical Implications

Jesus' humanity has several practical implications for believers:

- Empathy: Knowing that Jesus experienced human life allows believers to approach Him with confidence, seeking empathy and help in times of need (Hebrews 4:15-16).

- Moral Exemplar: Jesus' life sets a standard for ethical and moral living. His responses to temptation and suffering provide a roadmap for believers navigating the complexities of life.

- Incarnational Living: Jesus' example encourages Christians to live incarnational, meaning engaging deeply in the world while maintaining a commitment to God's standards.

The humanity of Jesus Christ is not merely a theological assertion but a profound reality that affects every aspect of Christian faith and practice. His life as a fully human individual who experienced the breadth of human life without sin provides a foundation for our redemption, a model for our lives, and a source of comfort in our struggles. By truly understanding and embracing Jesus' humanity, believers can more fully appreciate the depth of His sacrifice and the breadth of His empathy for us.

BIBLICAL EVIDENCE FOR JESUS' HUMAN EXPERIENCES AND EMOTIONS

The humanity of Jesus Christ is vividly portrayed throughout the New Testament, not only through His physical needs and biological relationships but profoundly through His emotional life and experiences. This chapter explores various scriptural passages that underscore the depth and breadth of Jesus' human experiences and emotions, providing believers with a richer understanding of how fully He participated in the human condition.

Physical Experiences of Jesus

1. Hunger and Thirst: Jesus experienced hunger after fasting for forty days and nights in the wilderness (Matthew 4:2). During His crucifixion, He expressed His thirst, a fundamental human need, saying, "I thirst" (John 19:28).

2. Fatigue: Jesus' physical fatigue is noted when He fell asleep in a boat amidst a storm, demonstrating His need for rest just like any other human (Mark 4:38).

3. Suffering and Death: The crucifixion of Jesus is the ultimate testament to His humanity. He endured physical torture and the excruciating pain of crucifixion, culminating in His human death (Mark 15:37).

Emotional Experiences of Jesus

1. Compassion: Jesus frequently felt compassion for the people around Him. For instance, seeing the crowds harassed and helpless, He felt compassion because they were like sheep without a shepherd (Matthew 9:36).

2. Joy: Jesus expressed joy, such as when He rejoiced in the Holy Spirit and thanked the Father for revealing truths to the simple-hearted instead of the wise (Luke 10:21).

3. Anger and Frustration: Jesus showed anger and frustration, notably when He cleansed the Temple by overturning the tables of the money changers and driving out merchants, demonstrating His zeal for God's house (John 2:15-17).

4. Sadness and Grief: Perhaps the most profound expression of His sadness is when Jesus wept at the tomb of Lazarus, showing His deep sorrow over the death of His friend and the pain it caused to Lazarus' family (John 11:35).

5. Anxiety and Distress: On the night before His crucifixion, Jesus experienced extreme anxiety and distress, as described in the Garden of Gethsemane. He expressed to His disciples, "My soul is exceedingly sorrowful, even to death" (Matthew 26:38).

Theological Implications of Jesus' Human Emotions

1. Relatability: Jesus' wide range of emotions makes Him relatable to us; He understands our experiences from the inside, not just as a divine observer. This relatability is critical for believers who seek a personal relationship with a God who truly knows what it is to be human.

2. Perfect Mediator: The full range of Jesus' emotions and experiences underscores His role as a perfect mediator. He has experienced the breadth of human feelings and can thus intercede on our behalf with genuine empathy (Hebrews 4:15).

3. Sinless Yet Emotional: Importantly, Jesus experienced all these emotions without sin. His anger was righteous, His sorrow was without despair, His joy was without frivolity. This perfection in emotional expression provides a model for believers on how to handle emotions righteously.

The biblical record of Jesus' human experiences and emotions is essential for understanding His full humanity. These experiences affirm that He was not merely a spiritual being temporarily wearing a human body but truly one of us, sharing in every aspect of human life. Through His life, believers are invited not only to relate to Him but also to emulate His sinless ways of experiencing and expressing human emotions. Understanding and reflecting on Jesus' emotional life can profoundly impact how we live, pray, and relate to God and one another, fostering a deeper, more empathetic Christian life.

THE IMPLICATIONS OF JESUS' HUMANITY FOR UNDERSTANDING SIN

The humanity of Jesus Christ is a fundamental doctrine that deeply influences Christian understanding of sin, temptation, and redemption. This chapter explores how Jesus' human experiences, particularly His temptations and sinless life, provide profound insights into the nature of sin and the human condition.

Jesus' Temptations and Sinlessness

1. The Temptation in the Wilderness: One of the most significant moments that highlight Jesus' humanity is His temptation by Satan in the wilderness (Matthew 4:1-11). Despite being hungry and weak after fasting for forty days, Jesus resists Satan's temptations. Each refusal reinforces the possibility of human obedience to God's will even under extreme conditions.

2. Sinless Yet Tempted: Hebrews 4:15 emphasizes that Jesus was "tempted in all points like as we are, yet without sin." This aspect of Jesus' life is crucial as it shows that being tempted is not a sin in itself; sin only results when one yields to temptation. Jesus' response to temptation sets a model for believers on how to confront and overcome sin.

Theological Implications

1. Understanding Human Frailty: Jesus' temptations reveal that human frailty can be met with divine strength. His reliance on Scripture to counter temptations (Matthew 4:4, 7, 10) demonstrates the power of God's Word in overcoming sin.

2. Nature of Sin and Temptation: By resisting sin, Jesus shows that temptation itself is not sinful—it is a common human experience. His victory over temptation provides insight into the nature of sin and God's expectations of humanity. Sin emerges not from the presence of temptation but from consenting to it.

3. The Role of Free Will: Jesus' choices during His life illustrate the role of free will in ethical and moral decisions. His sinlessness amidst temptation underscores the Christian belief that humans, while impaired by sin, are still capable of choosing good with the help of divine grace.

Practical Applications for Believers

1. Empathy and Forgiveness: Understanding that Jesus experienced temptation helps believers empathize with others who struggle with sin. This knowledge fosters a more compassionate and forgiving community, reflecting Jesus' own responses to those who erred.

2. Moral Responsibility: Jesus' life challenges believers to take responsibility for their actions. It inspires a pursuit of holiness and righteousness, grounded not in human strength but in the empowerment provided by the Holy Spirit.

3. Model of Victory Over Sin: Jesus is not only a sympathetic figure but also a victorious one. He provides not just a moral example but a practical pathway to overcoming sin through reliance on God's word and prayer.

Christological and Soteriological Significance

1. Christological: Jesus' full humanity is essential for His role as a mediator. Only someone who has experienced human life fully can truly represent humans before God. Jesus' experiences make Him the perfect advocate because He understands human weaknesses from personal experience.

2. Soteriological: The implications of Jesus' humanity extend to the very nature of salvation. His victory over sin and death as a human being is what qualifies Him to be the Savior. Through His humanity, the effects of sin are reversed, providing a way back to God that is grounded in empathy and justice.

The humanity of Jesus Christ has profound implications for Christian theology, particularly in understanding sin and redemption. His life demonstrates that it is possible to live a sinless life through reliance on God, despite the ubiquity of temptation. For believers, Jesus' human experiences and His triumph over sin offer not only a model to emulate but also a source of hope and assurance in the journey toward spiritual maturity and moral integrity. This deeper understanding of Jesus' humanity enriches the Christian faith, encouraging a life that is both empathetic towards human weakness and committed to divine standards.

THE HYPOTHETICAL: IMPLICATIONS IF JESUS COULD HAVE COMMITTED SINS

The sinlessness of Jesus Christ is central to Christian theology, directly impacting doctrines concerning His nature, the atonement, and His role as the perfect mediator between God and humanity. This chapter explores the hypothetical scenario where Jesus could have committed sins, examining the theological, soteriological, and ethical implications such a possibility would entail.

Theological Implications

1. Nature of Christ: The sinlessness of Jesus is integral to His identity as both fully human and fully divine. If Jesus had sinned, it would undermine the doctrine of His divinity, as sin is inherently contrary to God's nature. God's holiness and purity do not allow for sin, and thus, a sinful Jesus would contradict the essential attributes of God.

2. Trinitarian Harmony: The unity and coherence within the Trinity would also be challenged. The Father, Son, and Holy Spirit are one in nature and essence, sharing perfect holiness. Any sin in the person of Jesus would introduce a discord that is theologically irreconcilable with the unity and purity of the Trinity.

Soteriological Implications

1. Atonement and Redemption: Central to the work of salvation is the belief that Jesus, as the sinless sacrifice, died to atone for the sins of humanity. If Jesus had committed sins, His death could not serve as a vicarious atonement because He would need redemption Himself. A sinner cannot redeem other sinners; only a sinless person can offer a perfect sacrifice acceptable to God.

2. Mediatorial Role: In 1 Timothy 2:5, Jesus is described as the mediator between God and humans. His qualification for this role hinges on His sinlessness. A sinful mediator would not be able to stand before God on behalf of humanity, as His sin would disqualify Him from interceding effectively.

Ethical and Practical Implications

1. Moral Example: Jesus is considered the ultimate role model for righteousness and holy living. If He had sinned, His life would not serve as the perfect model for

believers. The ethical teachings of Jesus, which include calls to perfection and holiness, would lose their authority and effectiveness.

2. Faith and Worship: The worship of Jesus as God and the faith placed in His teachings and actions are predicated on His sinlessness. If He were not sinless, the validity of Christian faith and the legitimacy of worship directed towards Jesus would be severely compromised.

Philosophical and Doctrinal Considerations

1. Problem of Evil and Free Will: The hypothetical sinfulness of Jesus would also raise complex issues regarding the problem of evil and free will. It would necessitate a reevaluation of how divine foreknowledge and human free will interact, especially concerning the incarnate Son of God.

2. Incarnational Theology: The entire framework of incarnational theology, which hinges on the union of divine and human natures in Christ, would need rethinking. The implications of a sin-capable Jesus would challenge the foundational Christian understanding of what it means for God to become man.

While purely hypothetical, considering the possibility of Jesus committing sins helps underscore the critical importance of His sinlessness in Christian theology. Such speculation not only reaffirms the essential doctrines of the faith but also deepens the appreciation of the unique and holy nature of Jesus Christ. His sinlessness is not merely a doctrinal point but a cornerstone that supports the entire edifice of Christian belief and practice. This understanding prompts a deeper reflection on the significance of Jesus' purity and its impact on every aspect of faith, from personal sanctification to communal worship and theological integrity.

CHAPTER 03

THE DIVINITY OF JESUS CHRIST

The divinity of Jesus Christ is a cornerstone of Christian theology, asserting that Jesus is not only fully human but also fully divine. This chapter explores the scriptural foundations, theological implications, and the significance of Jesus' divine nature within the broader context of Christian doctrine and practice.

Scriptural Foundations of Jesus' Divinity

1. Prologue of John: John 1:1-14 states, "In the beginning was the Word, and the Word was with God, and the Word was God." This passage not only affirms Jesus' existence at the beginning of time but also unequivocally declares His Godhood, emphasizing His active role in creation and His incarnation as the life and light of humanity.

2. Divine Titles: Throughout the New Testament, Jesus is ascribed titles that signify His divine status. These include "Lord" (Philippians 2:11), "Son of God" (John 5:25),

and "Immanuel" (Matthew 1:23), which means "God with us." Each title carries with it implications of divine sovereignty, authority, and presence.

3. Miracles as Divine Acts: Jesus performed numerous miracles, such as turning water into wine (John 2:1-11), calming the storm (Mark 4:39-41), and raising the dead (John 11:43-44). These acts are not just proofs of divine power but also symbolic assertions of His control over the natural and supernatural realms.

4. Authority to Forgive Sins: In Mark 2:5-7, Jesus forgives the sins of a paralyzed man, a prerogative assumed to belong only to God. His ability to forgive sins not only demonstrates His divine authority but also visibly confirms His identity as God in human form.

5. Resurrection and Ascension: The resurrection of Jesus (Luke 24:1-7) and His ascension (Acts 1:9-11) are pivotal events that affirm His divinity. These acts validate His victory over death and His ultimate authority over heaven and earth.

Theological Implications of Jesus' Divinity

1. Trinitarian Doctrine: Jesus' divinity is central to the doctrine of the Trinity, which posits one God in three persons: Father, Son, and Holy Spirit. Understanding Jesus as

fully divine allows for a coherent theological framework in which the Trinity operates in unity and diversity.

2. Incarnation: The incarnation is the event of God becoming man. This doctrine hinges on the divine nature of Jesus, who, while taking on human flesh, maintained His divine essence. This mysterious union of human and divine natures in one person is what makes salvation possible.

3. Atonement: Only a divine savior could adequately bear the infinite weight of humanity's sins and offer a sacrifice sufficient to satisfy divine justice. Jesus' divine nature ensures that His death on the cross was efficacious for the redemption of all who believe in Him.

Significance for Christian Life and Worship

1. Worship and Devotion: Recognizing Jesus as divine shapes the worship and devotion of Christians, directing prayer, praise, and adoration towards Him as God. Worship that is due only to God is rightly directed to Jesus, reflecting His divine status.

2. Model of Perfect Love and Holiness: Jesus embodies the perfect love and holiness of God. Believers are called to emulate His character, which provides a divine model for living a life of righteousness and love.

3. Assurance of Salvation: The divinity of Jesus offers believers assurance that their salvation is secure, grounded not

in human effort but in the divine promise and power of God through Christ.

The divinity of Jesus Christ is not merely a theological abstract but a living reality that impacts every aspect of the Christian faith. It assures believers of the profound truth that in Jesus, God has indeed come near, offering redemption, demanding worship, and providing a divine example for living. This chapter affirms that understanding Jesus as 100% divine is essential for grasping the full scope of Christian doctrine and deeply influences how believers live out their faith in the world.

BIBLICAL EVIDENCE FOR JESUS' DIVINE ATTRIBUTES AND ACTIONS THE INCARNATION OF CHRIST

The divinity of Jesus Christ is a fundamental aspect of Christian theology, underpinning doctrines such as the Trinity, the Incarnation, and salvation. This chapter examines specific biblical passages that highlight Jesus' divine attributes and actions, underscoring His identity as God incarnate.

Divine Attributes of Jesus

1. Omnipotence: Jesus demonstrated His omnipotence through miracles that defy natural laws. For example, He calmed a raging storm on the Sea of Galilee with

a mere command: "Peace, be still" (Mark 4:39). His disciples reacted with awe, saying, "What manner of man is this, that even the wind and the sea obey him?"

2. Omniscience: Jesus exhibited knowledge that only God could possess. John 2:24-25 notes, "But Jesus did not commit himself unto them, because he knew all men, And needed not that any should testify of man: for he knew what was in man." This insight into human hearts is further displayed when He told Nathanael he had seen him under the fig tree before Philip called him (John 1:48).

3. Eternal Existence: Jesus spoke of His existence before Abraham, a patriarch who lived centuries earlier. In John 8:58, Jesus declares, "Verily, verily, I say unto you, Before Abraham was, I am." This statement not only claims pre-existence but also intentionally echoes the divine name "I AM" revealed to Moses in Exodus 3:14, indicating His eternal nature.

Divine Actions of Jesus

1. Creation: The prologue of the Gospel of John attributes creation to Jesus, stating, "All things were made by him; and without him was not any thing made that was made" (John 1:3). This role in creation is traditionally reserved for God alone, indicating Jesus' divine agency.

2. Forgiveness of Sins: Only God can forgive sins, a divine prerogative that Jesus exercised during His ministry. Mark 2:5-7 recounts Jesus telling a paralytic, "Son, thy sins be forgiven thee," which prompts religious leaders to question, "Who can forgive sins but God only?" This incident underscores His divine authority to absolve sin.

3. Resurrection and Life: Jesus not only raised others from the dead, as seen in the raising of Lazarus (John 11:43-44), but He also claimed the power to raise Himself. In John 10:17-18, He says, "I lay down my life, that I might take it again. No man taketh it from me, but I lay it down of myself. I have the power to lay it down, and I have the power to take it again." This assertion of power over life and death highlights His divine sovereignty.

4. Transcendence and Immanence: Jesus' ability to be both present with His disciples and yet omnipresent is a divine attribute. Before His ascension, He promised perpetual presence with His followers, saying, "Lo, I am with you always, even unto the end of the world" (Matthew 28:20). This promise indicates His divine attribute of omnipresence.

Theological Significance

Each of these attributes and actions is not merely a display of power but serves a deeper theological purpose. They reveal God's nature through Christ and confirm the claims of His divinity. These divine features assure believers of His sufficient authority and ability to accomplish salvation and sustain His church.

The biblical evidence for Jesus' divine attributes and actions is extensive and forms a central pillar of Christian faith. Understanding and affirming Jesus' divinity based on these scriptural attestations is crucial for believers. It shapes their worship, informs their theology, and provides comfort and assurance in the efficacy of Christ's sacrificial work on the cross. By recognizing Jesus as God, believers engage more deeply with the profound mystery and grace of the Christian gospel.

THE THEOLOGICAL IMPLICATIONS OF JESUS' DIVINITY ABOUT SINLESSNESS

The divinity of Jesus Christ is a defining pillar of Christian theology, intricately linked to his sinlessness. This chapter explores how Jesus' divine nature underpins his sinless life, examining the theological implications of this relationship for concepts such as atonement, redemption, and the human condition.

Understanding Jesus' Sinlessness

1. Biblical Foundation: Scripture asserts the sinlessness of Jesus as a fundamental aspect of his character.

Hebrews 4:15 describes Jesus as "tempted in all ways as we are, yet without sin." This sinlessness is essential not only for his role as a redeemer but also as a testament to his divine nature.

2. Divine Nature and Sinlessness: Jesus' divinity provides the foundation for his sinless nature. As God, Jesus embodies perfection and holiness, attributes that are incompatible with sin. The divine nature is inherently holy and free from the corruption that sin represents, which is why Jesus, being fully divine, is inherently sinless.

Theological Implications

1. Qualification for Atonement: One of the primary implications of Jesus' sinlessness, rooted in his divinity, is his qualification to serve as the perfect sacrificial lamb for humanity's sins. Only a sinless sacrifice could fully satisfy divine justice and offer reconciliation between God and man. His divine nature ensures the infinite value of his sacrificial death, making it sufficient to atone for the sins of the entire world.

2. Mediatorial Role: Jesus' unique position as both fully divine and fully human allows him to act as an effective mediator between God and humanity. His divinity ensures his ability to represent God perfectly, while his humanity allows him to represent man. His sinlessness, underscored by his

divinity, legitimizes his role as a mediator who can truly reconcile two parties estranged by sin.

3. Impeccability: The doctrine of impeccability posits that Jesus was not only sinless but, due to his divine nature, was incapable of sinning. This aspect emphasizes the perfection of Jesus' moral and spiritual character, strengthening the Christian understanding of him as a reliable and flawless redeemer and leader.

4. Example for Believers: Jesus' sinless life, underscored by his divine attributes, provides the ultimate model for holiness and ethical living. While believers cannot achieve sinlessness on their own, the example of Jesus, combined with the empowering presence of the Holy Spirit, guides and motivates a life striving toward godliness.

5. Assurance of Salvation: Jesus' divinity and sinlessness offer believers confidence in the effectiveness and permanence of their salvation. Because the sinless, divine Savior has secured their redemption, they can rest assured that their salvation is not based on their own fluctuating moral successes but on the steadfast righteousness of Christ.

The divinity of Jesus Christ and his resultant sinlessness are not merely doctrinal points but are central to the Christian faith's understanding of salvation, mediation, and sanctification. These qualities ensure that Jesus is the perfect savior, capable of rescuing humanity from sin and restoring them to a right relationship with God. For believers, Jesus' sinless, divine nature is not only a source of theological assurance but also a profound motive for spiritual devotion and ethical conduct. In contemplating the sinlessness of Jesus, Christians find both a challenge to emulate his holiness and comfort in his complete sufficiency as their redeemer. This chapter highlights the inextricable link between Jesus' divinity and his sinlessness, reinforcing the depth and richness of the salvation he offers.

COMPARING THE SINLESS OF ADAM AND EVE WITH JESUS' SINLESS NATURE

Before the Fall, Adam and Eve possessed a sinless nature, akin to the perpetual sinlessness demonstrated by Jesus Christ during His earthly ministry. This chapter explores the similarities between the initial sinlessness of humanity as represented by Adam and Eve and the enduring sinlessness of Jesus, drawing theological insights from these comparisons.

Initial Sinlessness of Adam and Eve

1. Created in God's Image: Adam and Eve were created in the image of God (Genesis 1:26-27), endowed with purity and innocence. This initial state reflects God's holiness

and His intention for humanity to live in perfect harmony with His will, free from sin.

2. Moral Integrity and Freedom: In their original state, Adam and Eve possessed moral integrity and the freedom to choose obedience to God. Their sinlessness was contingent upon their choices, underpinned by the freedom to obey or disobey God's commandments.

Jesus' Perpetual Sinlessness

1. Divine Nature: Unlike Adam and Eve, Jesus' sinlessness is anchored in His divine nature as the Son of God. Being fully divine, Jesus possessed an intrinsic holiness that could not be tainted by sin (Hebrews 7:26). His sinlessness was not just a state but an integral part of His being.

2. Human Experience and Temptation: Despite being fully human and experiencing temptations (Hebrews 4:15), Jesus maintained His sinlessness throughout His life. Unlike Adam and Eve, whose sinlessness was compromised by yielding to temptation, Jesus' response to temptation reinforced His sinless nature.

Similarities in Sinlessness

1. Representation: Both Adam and Eve and Jesus represented humanity, but in different capacities. Adam and Eve were humanity's progenitors, representing the potential and failure of human beings to live sinlessly. In contrast, Jesus

represented the fulfillment of what humanity could ideally be—perfectly obedient and forever sinless.

2. Relational Purpose with God: The sinlessness of both Adam and Eve and Jesus was intended to facilitate unhindered fellowship with God. Sinlessness is a prerequisite for a direct and unbroken relationship with God, which was evident in the Garden of Eden before the Fall and exemplified by Jesus during His earthly ministry.

3. Role in God's Plan: The initial sinlessness of Adam and Eve was central to God's original plan for humanity—a life in a perfect and obedient relationship with Him. Jesus' enduring sinlessness was crucial for restoring that relationship through the atonement, highlighting His role as the "second Adam" (1 Corinthians 15:45-49), who succeeds where the first Adam failed.

Differences in Sinlessness

1. Source of Sinlessness: Adam and Eve's sinlessness was derived from their created nature and was vulnerable to corruption. Conversely, Jesus' sinlessness was derived from His divine nature and remained incorruptible despite human temptations.

2. Impact of Sinlessness: The failure of Adam and Eve's sinlessness led to the Fall and the introduction of sin into the world, affecting all their descendants. In contrast,

Jesus maintained sinlessness achieved redemption, and offered salvation to all humanity, reversing the effects of the Fall.

The comparison between the sinlessness of Adam and Eve and that of Jesus Christ offers profound insights into the nature of sin, freedom, and redemption. While both represent states of sinlessness, the source, sustainability, and implications of their sinlessness diverge significantly, reflecting the overarching narrative of fall and redemption central to Christian theology. This analysis not only underscores the uniqueness of Jesus' sinlessness but also highlights its redemptive significance in the context of human history and divine salvation.

CHAPTER 04

THE SIN NATURE AND ORIGINAL SIN

In Christian theology, the concepts of sinful nature and original sin are fundamental in understanding the human condition and the need for divine salvation. This chapter explores the definitions, origins, and theological significance of these concepts, providing a comprehensive overview of how sin affects humanity and the implications for Christian belief and practice.

Definition of Sin Nature and Original Sin

1. Sin Nature: Sin nature refers to the inherent disposition towards sin that all humans possess. It is the internal inclination to rebel against God's laws and desires, manifesting in various sinful behaviors and attitudes. This nature is universally inherited by all people from their first parents, Adam and Eve.

2. Original Sin: Original sin specifically refers to the guilt and moral corruption passed down from Adam and Eve

following their transgression in the Garden of Eden. It is not merely the first sin committed but represents the fallen state that affects all humanity. This concept asserts that all humans are born into a condition of sinfulness that precedes actual sins committed.

Origins of the Sin Nature and Original Sin

1. The Fall of Adam and Eve: The origins of the sinful nature and original sin are traditionally traced back to the narrative of the Fall in Genesis 3. When Adam and Eve disobeyed God by eating the forbidden fruit, they not only committed the first sin but also altered the nature of human existence—spiritually corrupting themselves and their descendants.

2. Theological Interpretation: The Apostle Paul elaborates on this event in Romans 5:12-19, explaining that through one man's disobedience, many were made sinners. This passage has been foundational in developing the doctrine of original sin, emphasizing that the consequences of the Fall were not limited to Adam and Eve but extended to all humanity.

Theological Implications

1. Universal Sinfulness: The doctrine of original sin underscores the universal nature of sinfulness, asserting that all individuals are born with a sinful nature. This universality

is crucial for understanding the scope of salvation needed and offered through Jesus Christ.

2. Human Inability and Divine Grace: Because of sinful nature and original sin, humans are incapable of achieving righteousness on their own. This inability highlights the necessity of divine grace for salvation. It is only through God's intervention, particularly through the life, death, and resurrection of Jesus, that humanity can be redeemed.

3. Baptism and Regeneration: Within many Christian traditions, the doctrines of original sin and the sinful nature inform the practices and theology surrounding baptism. Baptism is often understood as a sacrament of regeneration, symbolically cleansing an individual from original sin and marking their rebirth into a new life in Christ.

4. Moral Responsibility and Free Will: Despite the inherent sinful nature, Christian theology also upholds the concepts of free will and moral responsibility. Believers are called to resist their sinful inclinations by the power of the Holy Spirit and to live in accordance with God's will.

The sin nature and original sin are central doctrines that address the human condition, offering explanations for the presence of evil and suffering in the world. They also form the backdrop against which the narrative of redemption unfolds, highlighting the transformative power of the gospel.

Understanding these concepts is crucial for grasping the depth of the human need for salvation and the profound nature of the grace offered through Jesus Christ. By acknowledging the reality of the sin nature and original sin, believers can more fully appreciate the significance of their redemption and the ongoing call to holiness in their lives.

BIBLICAL TEACHINGS ON ORIGINAL SIN AND ITS TRANSMISSION

Original sin, a pivotal doctrine in Christian theology, addresses the inherent sinfulness that afflicts humanity due to the first transgression by Adam and Eve. This chapter examines the biblical foundations for the concept of original sin and its transmission through generations, providing scriptural insights and theological interpretations that have shaped Christian understanding of human nature and the necessity for redemption.

Scriptural Basis for Original Sin

1. Genesis Account: The doctrine of original sin finds its roots in the Genesis narrative of the Fall (Genesis 3). When Adam and Eve disobeyed God's command by eating from the Tree of the Knowledge of good and Evil, sin entered the world. This act did not merely affect them individually but had ramifications for all their descendants.

2. Pauline Theology: The Apostle Paul provides the most explicit theological exposition of original sin and its transmission. Romans 5:12 states, "Wherefore, as by one man sin entered into the world, and death by sin; and so death passed upon all men, for that all have sinned." Paul argues that Adam's sin brought death and sin to all humanity, establishing a theological basis for the universal need for salvation.

Mechanisms of Transmission

1. Seminal Nature: One traditional interpretation, based on Hebrew conceptions of procreation, is that all humans were seminally present in Adam. Thus, when Adam sinned, all humanity sinned with him. This view is often associated with Augustine's writings, which have significantly influenced Western Christian thought.

2. Federal Headship: Another theological perspective is the federal headship, where Adam is considered the representative of all humanity. His actions, therefore, have legal and moral implications for all people, much like a covenant leader whose decisions bind the whole group.

Theological Implications and Interpretations

1. Total Depravity: The concept of original sin is closely linked with the doctrine of total depravity, which posits that every part of human nature is tainted by sin,

affecting thoughts, emotions, and behaviors. This condition underscores the comprehensive impact of sin on human nature and the profound need for divine grace for salvation.

2. Universal Guilt and Death: According to Romans 5:18-19, just as sin and death came through Adam, righteousness, and life come through Christ. This parallel establishes the universality of guilt from Adam contrasted with the universal offer of salvation through Jesus.

3. Infant Baptism: In many Christian traditions, the doctrine of original sin is used to justify the practice of infant baptism. The sacrament is seen as a means of washing away the original sin, marking the entry of the child into the Christian community, and initiating the process of sanctification.

Challenges and Contemporary Views

1. Historical-Critical Perspectives: Modern biblical scholarship often challenges traditional interpretations of original sin, suggesting that Paul's arguments in Romans were specific to his theological and cultural context and may not have intended to establish a doctrine of universal sin transmission.

2. Eastern Orthodox Perspective: The Eastern Orthodox Church does not embrace the concept of original sin as inherited guilt but views it as an inherited condition of

mortality and corruption. This perspective emphasizes the loss of communion with God rather than inherited guilt.

The doctrine of original sin is fundamental in Christian theology as it explains the universal human condition of sinfulness and the essential need for Christ's redemptive work. While interpretations vary among different Christian traditions, the scriptural teachings on original sin offer profound insights into human nature, the impact of sin, and God's gracious provision for salvation. Understanding these biblical teachings helps believers comprehend the depth of human sin and the breadth of divine grace, encouraging a life continually oriented towards repentance and renewal in Christ.

THE THEOLOGICAL DEBATE ON WHETHER JESUS INHERITED THE SIN NATURE

One of the most profound theological questions in Christian doctrine concerns whether Jesus Christ, being fully human, inherited the sinful nature that affects all of humanity. This chapter delves into the biblical basis, historical perspectives, and contemporary debates surrounding this issue, exploring how different theological traditions address the question of Jesus' sinlessness and human nature.

Biblical Basis

1. Hebrews 4:15: This verse is central to the discussion: "For we have not a high priest which cannot be touched with the feeling of our infirmities; but was in all points tempted like as we are, yet without sin." This passage asserts that while Jesus was tempted in every way common to humanity, He did not sin, suggesting a unique human nature.

2. Luke 1:35: The angel's announcement to Mary states, "The Holy Ghost shall come upon thee, and the power of the Highest shall overshadow thee: therefore also that holy thing which shall be born of thee shall be called the Son of God." The term "that holy thing" indicates that Jesus was sanctified from conception, set apart from the sinful nature.

Historical Perspectives

1. The Early Church: Early church fathers, including Athanasius and Augustine, debated the nature of Jesus' humanity and how it was free from the corruption of sin. They emphasized the Virgin Birth as key to understanding how Jesus avoided inheriting Adam's sin.

2. Council of Ephesus (431 AD): This council affirmed that Jesus was born of the Virgin Mary, who is proclaimed Theotokos, meaning "God-bearer," suggesting a special, sanctified conception that prevented the transmission of original sin to Jesus.

Theological Interpretations

1. Impeccability vs. Peccability: The debate often centers on whether Jesus could not sin (impeccability) or merely did not sin (peccability). Those who argue for impeccability often link it to His divine nature, suggesting that His divinity ensured He could not sin. In contrast, proponents of peccability emphasize His genuine humanity, suggesting that His sinlessness was a result of moral victory rather than inherent incapacity to sin.

2. Federal Headship: Under this theological framework, Jesus is seen as the new Adam who comes to reverse Adam's failure. Just as Adam's sin brought corruption to all humanity, Christ's righteousness brings the possibility of life and righteousness to all (Romans 5:17-19). Thus, His nature had to be untouched by sin to effectively act as the second Adam.

Contemporary Theological Dialogue

1. Liberation and Feminist Theologies: These perspectives often question traditional doctrines around sinful nature and emphasize the fully human experience of Jesus, including the potential to sin, to highlight His solidarity with the marginalized and oppressed.

2. Evangelical Theology: Many in the evangelical tradition maintain a strong stance on the sinlessness of Christ

from conception, viewing this as essential for the efficacy of His atoning sacrifice.

The question of whether Jesus inherited the sinful nature touches on core issues of Christian soteriology and Christology. While the debate continues among various theological schools, the consensus remains that Jesus lived a sinless life, essential for His role as the perfect mediator and redeemer. Understanding this debate helps believers appreciate the depth of Jesus' sacrifice and the profound mystery of the Incarnation—God becoming fully human while remaining fully divine and without sin. This chapter aims to provide a thorough understanding of the complex theological debates surrounding Jesus' human nature and His sinlessness, encouraging deeper reflection and informed faith.

PECCABILITY VS. IMPECCABILITY OF JESUS

Before we delve into the finer points of the ongoing theological debate between peccability and impeccability, it is crucial to first define the terms we are discussing.

First, peccability stems from the adjective "peccable," which is defined as 'liable to sin or error.' To add depth to this definition, it's noted that in the U.S., "peccable" can also mean 'susceptible to temptation.' These two definitions suggest nuances worth considering: being "liable to sin" implies a possibility and likelihood of sinning, whereas being "susceptible to temptation" does not necessarily indicate the likelihood of sinning, but rather a vulnerability to being tempted.

Second, impeccability is defined as 'faultless, flawless, irreproachable, not liable to sin.' Further enriched by the U.S. interpretation, it includes 'incapable of sinning.' The distinction between not being liable to sin and being incapable of sinning, though subtle in phrasing, is significant in meaning.

To contextualize these definitions within a biblical framework, we turn to Scripture that illustrates the concepts of sin, temptation, and moral perfection. James 1:13-15 provides insight into the nature of temptation and sin: "Let no man say when he is tempted, I am tempted of God: for God cannot be tempted with evil, neither tempteth he any man: But every man is tempted, when he is drawn away of his own lust, and enticed. Then when lust hath conceived, it bringeth forth sin: and sin, when it is finished, bringeth forth death." This passage clarifies that God Himself is impeccable, being incapable of sin or temptation, setting a divine standard against which human peccability is contrasted.

Hebrews 4:15 further elaborates on Jesus' unique nature in relation to temptation and sin: "For we have not a high priest which cannot be touched with the feeling of our infirmities; but was in all points tempted like as we are, yet without sin." This verse highlights that while Jesus was susceptible to the experience of temptation—aligning with the human condition—He remained sinless, supporting the doctrine of His impeccability.

Thus, understanding these theological terms within the biblical context not only enriches our grasp of the nature of Christ but also deepens our understanding of the human condition in relation to sin and redemption.

Now we turn to the inerrant, inspired, ineffable, and infallible Word of God. When considering the moral character of our Lord and Savior, a standout verse for many is 1 Peter 2:22, which states:

'He committed no sin, neither was deceit found in his mouth.'

This passage from Peter is unequivocal; Jesus Christ committed no sin and was never deceitful in word or deed.

Isaiah 53:9 further corroborates this, describing our Lord and Savior as follows:

'And they made his grave with the wicked and with a rich man in his death, although he had done no violence, and there was no deceit in his mouth.'

Commenting on this verse, David Guzik notes, "The line 'because He had done no violence, nor was any deceit in His mouth' is important. It shows that even in His death, even in His taking the transgressions of God's people, the Messiah never sinned. He remained the Holy One, despite all the pain and suffering."

Several other Scriptures affirm the sinless nature of Jesus, the spotless Lamb of God:

2 Corinthians 5:21:

'For our sake, he made him to be sin who knew no sin, so that in him we might become the righteousness of God.'

This verse highlights the profound mystery of the atonement, where Jesus, who was without sin, was made to be sin for us, offering us His righteousness in exchange.

Hebrews 4:15:

'For we do not have a high priest who is unable to sympathize with our weaknesses, but one who in every respect has been tempted as we are, yet without sin.'

Here, we see that Jesus, while fully experiencing the breadth of human temptation, remained without sin, making Him the perfect mediator who understands our struggles yet is wholly pure.

Hebrews 7:26:

'For it was indeed fitting that we should have such a high priest, holy, innocent, unstained, separated from sinners, and exalted above the heavens.'

This passage describes the transcendent holiness of Jesus, emphasizing His purity and separation from sin, which qualifies Him uniquely as our high priest.

1 John 3:5:

'You know that he appeared in order to take away sins, and in him there is no sin.'

John reaffirms that the purpose of Jesus' manifestation was to remove sin, a mission only possible because He Himself was without sin.

These scriptural affirmations provide a robust foundation for understanding the sinless nature of Jesus. They not only affirm His moral perfection but also enrich our appreciation for the magnitude of His sacrifice and the depth of His love, compelling us as believers to live in light of this profound truth.

The question of whether Jesus Christ could have sinned, known as the debate between peccability (the ability to sin) and impeccability (the inability to sin), is more than a theological curiosity—it strikes at the heart of Christ's nature and His qualifications as our High Priest. While it is clear and biblically affirmed that Jesus did not commit sin, the question remains about the theoretical possibility of sinning.

Biblical Context and Doctrine

The foundational scripture for this discussion is Hebrews 4:15, which states:

"For we do not have a high priest who is unable to sympathize with our weaknesses, but one who in every respect has been tempted as we are, yet without sin."

This verse underlines Jesus' full humanity in experiencing temptation, yet His divine nature remains untainted by sin. To explore this, we must delve into the implications of Jesus' temptations and His sinless response.

The Argument for Peccability

Those advocating for peccability argue that for Jesus' temptations to be genuine, there must have been a real possibility of Him yielding to these temptations. The reality of temptation, they suggest, implies the possibility of failure; otherwise, the temptations would seem to be mere illusions without real moral or spiritual stakes.

Charles Hodge, a prominent theologian, articulates this view, stating:

"This sinlessness of our Lord, however, does not amount to absolute impeccability... If He was a true man, He must have been capable of sinning... Temptation implies the possibility of sin. If from the constitution of his person it was impossible for Christ to sin, then his temptation was unreal and without effect, and He cannot sympathize with his people."

The Argument for Impeccability

On the other side, proponents of impeccability argue that Jesus' divine nature and His role as the sinless Lamb of God made it impossible for Him to sin. This perspective does not diminish the reality or seriousness of His temptations; rather, it emphasizes His divine perfection and the purpose of these temptations.

The impeccability argument is framed around the idea that Jesus' temptations were not to see if He could sin, but to prove that He could not. His sinlessness was a demonstration of His divine nature and mission to overcome sin on behalf of humanity.

Hebrews 4:15 Explained

Examining Hebrews 4:15, we see that Jesus was "tempted as we are, yet without sin." This implies that while He experienced temptation in all the ways humans do, His response—sinlessness—was rooted in His unique nature as both God and man. The phrase "yet without sin" does not suggest He had a sin nature that He resisted; rather, it affirms His inherent holiness and separation from sin.

Conclusion: Theological and Practical Implications

The debate over peccability versus impeccability is not just academic. It touches on the very nature of Christ's empathy, His identification with human struggles, and His victory over sin. The understanding that Jesus faced real temptations yet did not sin provides profound comfort and assurance for believers. It shows that He truly understands human frailty and offers a model of victory over temptation and sin.

Ultimately, whether one leans toward the peccability or impeccability viewpoint, it is crucial to affirm the biblical truth of Jesus' sinlessness. His perfect response to temptation is what qualifies Him as our effective High Priest and Savior, making a way for us to approach God with confidence in His grace.

The doctrinal discussion surrounding whether Jesus could have sinned (peccability) versus His inability to sin (impeccability) often involves interpreting key scriptural terms and their theological implications. Central to this discussion is the understanding of the term 'sympathize' from the Greek 'sympatheō', and the concept of Jesus being 'tempted' as described in the pivotal verse, Hebrews 4:15.

Scriptural Foundations and Analysis

1. Sympathizing with Weaknesses: The Greek term 'sympatheō', translated as 'sympathize', encompasses meanings such as "to feel for" or "have compassion on." This suggests that Jesus' ability to sympathize with our weaknesses does not necessitate His having sinned; rather, His omniscience allows Him to fully understand human frailty and temptation, even without personally yielding to sin. This distinction is crucial in understanding His role as our High Priest, who intercedes with perfect empathy (Hebrews 4:15).

2. The Nature of Temptation: The Greek word 'peirazō' used in Hebrews 4:15, often translated as 'tempted', can mean "to test" or "to try" for the purpose of proving someone's quality or integrity. This supports the view that Jesus' temptations were real and challenging, intended to demonstrate His sinless character, not to see if He could fail.

- Hebrews 4:15: "For we do not have a high priest who is unable to sympathize with our weaknesses, but one who in every respect has been tempted as we are, yet without sin."

This verse underscores that while Jesus faced genuine temptations, His experiences did not lead to sin, affirming His impeccable nature.

Theological Interpretation and Orthodoxy

1. Temptations as Demonstrations: The temptations of Christ, particularly those in the wilderness (Luke 4:1-2, Matthew 4:1), orchestrated by the Holy Spirit, were not to ascertain if Jesus could sin but to prove His sinless and flawless character. According to James 1:13, "Let no one say when he is tempted, 'I am being tempted by God,' for God cannot be tempted with evil, and He himself tempts no one." This aligns with the understanding that God led Jesus into the wilderness not to tempt Him into sinning but to demonstrate His holiness and perfect obedience.

2. Implications of Jesus' Divine Nature: The full deity of Christ resided in Him during His earthly ministry, as stated in Colossians 1:19 and 2:9, which assert that the fullness of God was pleased to dwell in Him and that in Him the whole fullness of deity dwells bodily. Thus, to suggest that Jesus could have sinned is akin to suggesting that God could sin, directly contradicting Scriptures that declare God's perfect holiness (Psalm 92:15, Mark 10:18).

Concluding Thoughts on Christ's Sinlessness

The orthodox understanding, upheld since the Council of Chalcedon in 451, asserts that Jesus Christ is one person, fully God and fully man, without division or confusion between His natures. This Christological truth means that Jesus' divinity and humanity cannot be separated into parts where one might sin while the other could not. As H.C. Thiessen articulates in Lectures in Systematic Theology, Christ's unified nature as both God and man upholds His impeccability.

Jesus' ability to sympathize with our weaknesses, as our High Priest, does not imply a necessity for Him to have sinned. Rather, His experiences of temptation were real and profound, serving to prove His sinless nature and His qualification to intercede on our behalf. This understanding not only aligns with scriptural teachings but also offers profound comfort and assurance for believers, knowing that their Savior fully understands and compassionately intercedes for them without having succumbed to sin.

The theological inquiry into whether Jesus could have sinned, often revolves around understanding key scriptural terms such as 'sympathize' and 'tempted.' This discussion is anchored in the exploration of Jesus' complete submission to the will of God, evidencing His impeccability. Theologically and logically, it's difficult to reconcile the idea that God would incarnate, live sinlessly, die for humanity's sins, and yet entertain personal sin.

Scriptural Analysis and Commentary

1. Submission to God's Will: Scripture repeatedly highlights Jesus' submission to God's will as proof of His sinlessness and divine mission:

- Matthew 26:39, 42: In Gethsemane, Jesus prays, "Not as I will, but as you will," showcasing His commitment to God's will over His human desires.

- John 6:38: Jesus declares, "For I have come down from heaven not to do my will but to do the will of him who sent me," affirming His divine obedience.

- Hebrews 5:8: "Although he was a son, he learned obedience from what he suffered," illustrating that His experiences were designed to prove His sinlessness and obedience.

2. Understanding 'Sympatheō' and 'Peirazō':

- The Greek 'sympatheō' in Hebrews 4:15 translates as 'sympathize' and implies a deep, compassionate understanding of human weakness, not necessitating personal sin to empathize.

- 'Peirazō,' used for 'tempted,' suggests a testing of character rather than an enticement to sin, pointing to Jesus being tested as proof of His moral perfection and divine nature.

3. Orthodoxy and the Nature of Christ's Temptations:

- The temptations in the wilderness (Luke 4:1-2, Matthew 4:1) are viewed not as opportunities for sin but as demonstrations of Christ's sinless character.

- James 1:13 reinforces this, stating, "God cannot be tempted by evil, nor does he tempt anyone." This establishes that the Holy Spirit's leading into the wilderness was to demonstrate, not to doubt, Christ's impeccable nature.

4. Impeccability vs. Peccability:

- The argument for impeccability is strengthened by understanding that while Jesus was temptable due to His humanity, His divine nature and will were perfectly aligned with God's, making sin impossible. As Charles C. Ryrie explains in A Survey of Bible Doctrine, orthodox theology does not support a division or third nature in Christ; He remains fully God and fully man, indivisible and sinless.

5. Immutability and Impeccability:

- Hebrews 13:8, "Jesus Christ is the same yesterday and today and forever," supports the doctrine of immutability, suggesting that any potential for sin would contradict His unchanging divine nature.

- The implications are that Christ's divine attributes, including His inability to sin, are eternal, underscoring His role as a perfect mediator and savior.

The theological consensus, rooted deeply in Scripture, asserts that Christ's impeccability is not just about His lack of sin but about His inherent inability to sin, upheld by His divine nature and mission. The discussions surrounding His temptations and His ability to sympathize with human weaknesses do not imply a potential for sin but rather affirm His qualification as the perfect High Priest, capable of fully representing and redeeming humanity without blemish.

Thus, understanding Christ's impeccability is crucial not only for theological accuracy but also for appreciating the depth of His sacrifice and the perfection of His mediatorial work. This recognition allows believers to fully trust in His redemptive work and draw strength from His example of holy submission to God's will.

Understanding Christ's impeccable nature is not only a doctrinal necessity but also profoundly impactful for everyday Christian living. As elucidated in 1 Peter 1:14-21, the implications of Christ's eternal impeccability provide both a challenge and a comfort to believers.

Scriptural Insights and Personal Application

1 Peter 1:14-21 delineates the practical consequences of Jesus' sinlessness and His role as the sacrificial Lamb of God:

"As obedient children, do not be conformed to the passions of your former ignorance, but as he who called you is holy, you also be holy in all your conduct, since it is written, 'You shall be holy, for I am holy.' And if you call on him as Father who judges impartially according to each one's deeds, conduct yourselves with fear throughout the time of your exile, knowing that you were ransomed from the futile ways inherited from your forefathers, not with perishable things such as silver or gold, but with the precious blood of Christ, like that of a lamb without blemish or spot. He was foreknown before the foundation of the world but was made manifest in the last times for the sake of you who through him are believers in God, who raised him from the dead and gave him glory so that your faith and hope are in God."

Theological Reflections

- Christ's Appointment and Mission: Jesus was designated before the world's foundation to be the sinless and supreme sacrificial Lamb, necessary for the redemption of humanity. His impeccable nature underscores the reliability and effectiveness of His atonement, affirming that notions of His potential sinfulness are both unbiblical and theologically inaccurate.

- Call to Holiness: The passage calls believers to emulate the holiness of Christ in their daily conduct. Since

Jesus, who faced temptations yet remained sinless, has ransomed believers with His perfect sacrifice, we are urged to live not according to our old ways but in a manner that reflects His holy nature.

Practical Implications for Believers

- Understanding Jesus' Support: Knowing that Jesus is impeccable—that He faced temptations but remained undefiled—offers believers immense comfort and assurance. He understands our struggles not because He succumbed to them but because He overcame them.

- Reaching Out to Jesus: Christ's readiness to assist those who face temptations is profound. Believers are encouraged to approach Him for help and guidance, trusting that He is not only capable but also willing to provide the support needed to overcome sin and live righteously.

- Living in Reverence: The knowledge that we have been ransomed not with perishable things but with the precious blood of Christ should instill a deep sense of reverence and purpose in our lives. This recognition prompts believers to live in a way that honors the sacrifice made on their behalf.

Christ's impeccability has significant implications for every believer. It challenges us to live holy lives, free from past sins, and assures us of a Savior who understands and aids us in our weaknesses. As we continue to reflect on His sinless nature, let us strive to embody the holiness He exemplifies, reaching out to Him in faith and living with the confident hope placed in our impeccable Savior.

This understanding is not just a theological position but a transformative reality that should guide our daily actions, thoughts, and relationships, ensuring that our lives bear witness to the power and purity of Christ's sacrifice.

CHAPTER 05

SINLESSNESS OF JESUS

The sinlessness of Jesus Christ is a central tenet of Christian theology, pivotal for understanding His divine nature and His role as the perfect mediator and redeemer. This chapter explores the biblical evidence supporting Jesus' sinlessness, examining texts from both the New Testament and Old Testament prophecies, and discusses the implications of His sinless life for Christian doctrine and practice.

New Testament Affirmations

1. Gospels' Testimony: The Gospels consistently portray Jesus as a figure who, despite being tempted and tried in every way, remains without sin. Notably, in the temptation narratives (Matthew 4:1-11, Luke 4:1-13), Jesus resists all of Satan's enticements, using Scripture as His defense, thereby highlighting His adherence to God's will and His sinless nature.

2. Epistolary Evidence:

- Hebrews 4:15: This verse is often cited as definitive proof of Jesus' sinlessness: "For we do not have a high priest who is unable to empathize with our weaknesses, but we have one who has been tempted in every way, just as we are—yet he did not sin." This underscores His moral perfection and His capacity to intercede on behalf of sinners.

- 2 Corinthians 5:21: Paul's declaration that "For he hath made him to be sin for us, who knew no sin; that we might be made the righteousness of God in him," further cement the doctrine of Christ's sinlessness as fundamental to the Christian understanding of atonement.

- 1 Peter 2:22: Peter refers to Jesus by quoting Isaiah, saying, "Who did no sin, neither was guile found in his mouth." This attestation from an apostle and eyewitness of Jesus' life adds significant weight to the claim of His sinlessness.

Old Testament Prophecies

1. Isaiah's Servant Songs: Isaiah 53, one of the so-called Servant Songs, portrays a figure who, though suffering unjustly, does so without any deceit or sinfulness. "He had done no violence, neither was any deceit in his mouth" (Isaiah 53:9). Early Christians and New Testament writers understood these passages as referring to Jesus, viewing them as prophetic of His sinless sacrifice.

2. Psalms: Psalm 16:10, which is interpreted by Christians as prophetic of Jesus, states, "For you will not leave

my soul in Sheol, nor will you allow your Holy One to see corruption." This passage is often seen as indicating the holy (sinless) nature of the Messiah, who even in death, remains untouched by the corruption associated with sin.

Theological Implications

1. Atonement: Jesus' sinlessness is crucial for the Christian doctrine of atonement. Only a sinless sacrifice could adequately bear the sins of the world and satisfy the demands of divine justice. His sinlessness ensures that His death is sufficient and effective for the salvation of humanity.

2. Mediation: As a sinless mediator, Jesus bridges the gap between a holy God and sinful humanity. His unique position as both fully human and fully divine, coupled with His sinlessness, makes Him the perfect intermediary who can empathize with human weaknesses while advocating before God.

3. Moral Exemplar: Jesus' sinless life serves as the ultimate moral example for believers. His responses to temptation and suffering provide a model of perfect obedience to God's will, encouraging Christians to pursue holiness in their own lives.

The biblical evidence for the sinlessness of Jesus is comprehensive and forms a foundational aspect of His identity as recorded in Scripture. This sinlessness is not a peripheral attribute but a core quality that qualifies Him for His redemptive work and exemplary life. For believers, Jesus' sinlessness is both a doctrine to be affirmed and a reality to be reflected in their lives, encouraging them to live in a manner that honors His sacrificial love and divine holiness. This exploration of Jesus' sinlessness from scriptural, prophetic, and theological perspectives aims to deepen understanding and inspire greater faithfulness among followers of Christ.

THEOLOGICAL ARGUMENTS SUPPORTING JESUS' SINLESSNESS
THE INCARNATION OF CHRIST

The sinlessness of Jesus Christ is a cornerstone of Christian theology, essential for the doctrines of atonement, redemption, and Christ's mediatorial role. This chapter examines the theological arguments that support the sinlessness of Jesus, exploring how this attribute is integral to His identity and mission as the Son of God and Savior of the world.

Biblical Foundations

1. Divine Nature: Jesus' sinlessness is intrinsically linked to His divine nature. As God incarnate, Jesus shares in the holy and unblemished nature of God the Father. Since

God is inherently incapable of sinning due to His perfect holiness, so too is Jesus, who is God in human flesh (John 1:1, 14).

2. Virgin Birth: The virgin birth is often cited as a theological reason for Jesus' sinlessness. This miraculous event, as described in Matthew 1:18-25 and Luke 1:34-35, implies that Jesus did not inherit original sin through a human father. The Holy Spirit's role in His conception is seen as ensuring His purity from the moment of His incarnation.

3. Fulfillment of Old Testament Prophecy: Jesus is described as the sinless "servant" in Isaiah's prophecies (Isaiah 53:9). His fulfillment of these prophecies not only confirms His messianic identity but also His sinless nature, which is necessary for the atoning sacrifice prophesied in the Old Testament.

Theological Necessity of Sinlessness

1. Atoning Sacrifice: For the atonement to be effective, it had to be made by a sinless sacrifice. As sin creates separation from God, only a sinless individual could bridge this gap. Jesus' sinlessness makes His sacrificial death on the cross both sufficient and effective, satisfying divine justice and reconciling humanity with God (Hebrews 7:26-27).

2. Perfect Mediator: Jesus' role as mediator between God and humanity (1 Timothy 2:5) is predicated on His

sinlessness. Only someone who is both fully divine and fully human—and without sin—could mediate this relationship. His sinlessness ensures His ability to represent humanity before God without the need for His own atonement.

3. Moral Exemplar: Jesus serves as the ultimate example of holy living. His sinlessness provides a perfect model for believers to aspire to in their spiritual and moral lives (1 Peter 2:21-22). This aspect of His life is crucial for Christian ethics and the call to personal holiness.

Objections and Counterarguments

1. Human Experience: Some argue that if Jesus was truly human, He must have had the capacity to sin. Proponents of Jesus' sinlessness counter this by distinguishing between having the ability to be tempted (which Jesus had) and yielding to temptation (which He never did).

2. Peccability vs. Impeccability: The debate between whether Jesus could sin (peccability) versus could not sin (impeccability) centers around His free will. The orthodox position maintains that while Jesus was capable of being tempted, His divine nature and perfect union with the Father ensured He would not sin.

The theological arguments supporting Jesus' sinlessness are robust, drawing on scriptural evidence, doctrinal necessity, and the logical coherence of Christian theology. His sinlessness is fundamental not only for understanding the nature of the atonement but also for appreciating the depth of His sacrifice and the example He sets for believers. This chapter aims to articulate these arguments clearly, reinforcing the significance of Jesus' purity in the broader narrative of salvation and Christian life.

JESUS' TEMPTATIONS AND RESPONSES AS EVIDENCE OF HIS SINLESSNESS

The sinlessness of Jesus Christ is a central element of Christian theology, essential for understanding His divine mission and the efficacy of His atoning sacrifice. This chapter explores the accounts of Jesus' temptations, particularly those detailed in the Gospels of Matthew and Luke, to analyze how His responses during these trials serve as compelling evidence of His sinlessness.

Narratives of Temptation

1. The Wilderness Temptations: After fasting for forty days and nights in the wilderness, Jesus was tempted by Satan (Matthew 4:1-11, Luke 4:1-13). These temptations included turning stones into bread, throwing Himself from the temple to test God's protection, and worshiping Satan in exchange for the kingdoms of the world. Each temptation was designed

to exploit human weakness: physical hunger, spiritual pride, and power lust.

2. Gethsemane's Agony: Another poignant episode of temptation occurred in the Garden of Gethsemane (Matthew 26:36-46). Here, Jesus struggled with the imminent prospect of His suffering and crucifixion, praying for the cup of suffering to pass from Him yet submitting to the Father's will. This moment underscores His moral and spiritual resolve in the face of profound dread and anguish.

Analysis of Responses

1. Scriptural Recourse: In responding to the wilderness temptations, Jesus quoted Scripture as His defense, specifically citing passages from Deuteronomy. This method of response highlights His deep reverence for God's Word and His commitment to living in accordance with it, regardless of His physical or emotional state.

- Hunger Temptation: Jesus countered the suggestion to turn stones into bread with, "Man shall not live by bread alone, but by every word that proceeds from the mouth of God" (Matthew 4:4), emphasizing spiritual nourishment over physical.

- Temple Temptation: When urged to test God's protection, He replied, "It is written again, Thou shalt not tempt the Lord thy God" (Matthew 4:7), reinforcing His trust in and reverence for God's authority.

- Kingdoms Temptation: Confronted with the offer of worldly power, Jesus declared, "Get thee hence, Satan: for it is written, Thou shalt worship the Lord thy God, and him only shalt thou serve" (Matthew 4:10), affirming His unwavering devotion to God alone.

2. Submission to God's Will: In Gethsemane, despite His distress, Jesus submitted to God's will, stating, "O my Father, if this cup may not pass away from me, except I drink it, thy will be done" (Matthew 26:42). This submission, despite severe emotional and physical foreboding, demonstrates His perfect obedience and sinlessness.

Theological Significance

1. Model of Righteousness: Jesus' responses to temptation provide a model of righteousness for believers. He demonstrates that it is possible to resist temptation by relying on God's Word and maintaining submission to God's will.

2. Proof of Sinlessness: These narratives are crucial for establishing Jesus' sinlessness. His ability to resist all forms of temptation without sinning confirms His moral and spiritual perfection, qualifying Him as the perfect sacrificial lamb capable of atoning for the sins of humanity.

3. Empathetic High Priest: Hebrews 4:15 describes Jesus as a high priest who can sympathize with our weaknesses, having been tempted in every way, just as we are, yet without sin. His experiences allow Him to empathize with human struggles, making Him an effective mediator and advocate.

The temptations of Jesus and His impeccable responses are not merely historical anecdotes but foundational proofs of His sinlessness and divine mission. Through His reactions to each temptation, Jesus demonstrated His complete alignment with God's will and His utter rejection of sin. These episodes reinforce His role as the sinless Savior, whose life and actions provide both the basis for salvation and a template for Christian conduct. This chapter elucidates the depth of Jesus' commitment to righteousness and the profound implications of His sinlessness for all believers.

CHAPTER 06

HISTORICAL VIEWS ON JESUS' SINLESSNESS AND THE NATURE OF HIS HUMANITY AND DIVINITY

The sinlessness of Jesus Christ, along with the nature of His humanity and divinity, has been a focal point of theological reflection since the early days of Christianity. This chapter explores how various historical perspectives have shaped our understanding of these doctrines, examining the evolution of these ideas through the lenses of early church fathers, medieval theologians, and modern scholars.

Early Church Fathers

1. Apostolic Fathers: The immediate successors of the apostles, such as Ignatius of Antioch and Clement of Rome, emphasized Jesus' divinity and sinlessness in their writings, underscoring His role as the divine Savior who transcends the sinfulness of humanity.

2. Ante-Nicene Fathers: Early theologians like Justin Martyr and Irenaeus developed a more nuanced

understanding of Christ's nature. They defended the real humanity and divinity of Jesus against Gnostic teachings that denied His human nature.

3. Nicene and Post-Nicene Fathers: The debates culminated in the First Council of Nicaea (AD 325) and the Council of Chalcedon (AD 451), which affirmed the doctrine of Jesus as fully God and fully man. These councils articulated the belief in Jesus' sinlessness as part of His divine nature, while also stressing that His human nature was like ours in every respect except for being without sin.

Medieval Theologians

1. St. Augustine: Augustine's writings heavily influenced the Western Church's views on original sin and its transmission. He argued that Jesus was exempt from original sin, inheriting a human nature through the Virgin Mary that was not subject to Adam's corrupted lineage.

2. Thomas Aquinas: Aquinas offered a detailed analysis of Christ's nature in his Summa Theologica. He discussed how Jesus' human will was always perfectly aligned with His divine will, thereby maintaining His sinlessness. Aquinas also reinforced the Chalcedonian definition of Christ as one person with two natures, fully human and fully divine.

Reformation Perspectives

1. Martin Luther and John Calvin: The Reformers re-emphasized the sinlessness of Jesus as foundational to the doctrine of justification by faith. They saw Christ's righteous life as essential for His role as the perfect substitute for sinners. Luther's communicatio idiomatum theory posited that the attributes of both natures (divine and human) are ascribed to the single person of Christ.

2. Anabaptists and Radicals: While agreeing on the sinlessness of Jesus, they placed a greater emphasis on His human ability to resist temptation, viewing it as an example for believers to emulate through the power of the Holy Spirit.

Modern Theological Developments

1. Liberal Theology: In the 19th and 20th centuries, figures like Friedrich Schleiermacher and Albrecht Ritschl debated the implications of Jesus' sinlessness, often focusing more on His exemplary human moral achievements than on traditional notions of divine sinlessness.

2. Neo-Orthodoxy: Karl Barth and Dietrich Bonhoeffer, reacting against liberal theological trends, reasserted the traditional view of Jesus' sinlessness connected to His divine identity, emphasizing the mystery and transcendence involved in the Incarnation.

3. Contemporary Scholarly Debate: Modern theologians continue to explore the implications of Jesus'

sinlessness within the context of Christological debates, often focusing on the ethical and existential significance of His life and teachings.

Historical views on Jesus' sinlessness and the dual nature of His humanity and divinity have evolved but have always remained central to Christian theology. These doctrines are not merely academic but are crucial for understanding the nature of salvation, the character of Christ, and His relevance to human life and destiny. Each era's perspectives contribute layers of insight that enrich our ongoing dialogue about who Jesus is and what He means for humanity. This historical journey through theological thought provides a deep well of wisdom for contemporary believers seeking to understand and follow Jesus.

THE IMPACT OF JESUS' SINLESSNESS CHRISTIAN THEOLOGY AND SOTERIOLOGY

The sinlessness of Jesus Christ is not merely a doctrinal point but a profound truth that resonates throughout Christian theology and soteriology—the study of salvation. This chapter explores the far-reaching implications of Jesus' sinlessness, examining how this attribute affects doctrines of atonement, redemption, justification, and sanctification within the Christian faith.

Foundational Theological Implications

1. Nature of God and Christology: Jesus' sinlessness is crucial for maintaining the consistency of His divine nature with the holy and perfect nature of God. It affirms key Christological doctrines that Jesus is both fully God and fully man, capable of bridging the divine-human divide.

2. Trinitarian Relations: The sinlessness of Jesus supports the integrity of the Trinity, ensuring that His actions and experiences as the Son do not conflict with the holy nature of the Father and the Holy Spirit.

Soteriological Implications

1. Atonement: Central to Christian soteriology is the belief that Jesus' death on the cross provided the perfect sacrifice for sin. His sinlessness is essential because it means His sacrifice was not for His own sins (as He had none) but purely for the sins of humanity. This unblemished offering fulfills the Old Testament requirements for sacrificial lambs, which had to be without defect (Leviticus 22:20-22).

2. Justification: Pauline theology, particularly in Romans and Galatians, emphasizes that believers are justified by faith in Christ—His righteous, sinless life is imputed to them by faith. Jesus' sinlessness is foundational here; if He had sinned, He could not impart righteousness to believers.

3. Propitiation: Jesus' sinlessness allows Him to be the propitiation for our sins, absorbing the wrath of God that was due to us and restoring our relationship with the Father (1 John 2:2). This propitiatory role could only be fulfilled by someone who was Himself sinless.

4. Redemption and Ransom: Jesus' sinlessness ensures that He was a sufficient ransom for humanity, as taught in Mark 10:45. A sinful redeemer would have been inadequate to pay the price required to liberate humanity from the bondage of sin and death.

Practical and Ethical Implications

1. Moral Exemplar: As a sinless individual, Jesus serves as the ultimate moral example for Christians. His life provides a model of perfect obedience to God that believers are called to emulate (1 Peter 2:21-22). This is not only about avoiding sin but actively pursuing righteousness.

2. High Priestly Ministry: Hebrews highlights Jesus' ongoing ministry as a high priest who intercedes for believers before God (Hebrews 7:24-26). His sinlessness makes Him uniquely qualified for this role, as He can sympathize with human weaknesses without having been compromised by sin.

Theological Debates and Discussions

1. Peccability vs. Impeccability: The debate over whether Jesus could have sinned (peccability) or could not

have sinned (impeccability) touches directly on the nature of His temptations and His human will. While the question is complex, His sinlessness, however, understood, underscores His unique role in salvation history.

2. Historical and Cultural Context: Modern theologians often discuss the relevance of Jesus' sinlessness in contemporary cultural and social contexts, exploring how this doctrine influences Christian ethics and public morality in a pluralistic society.

The doctrine of Jesus' sinlessness is a cornerstone of Christian theology, intricately linked with every aspect of soteriology. It assures believers of the efficacy of Christ's work on the cross, undergirds their hope in eternal life, and guides their moral and ethical conduct. By understanding the depth and breadth of Jesus' sinlessness, believers gain a richer appreciation of the gospel's power and a clearer vision of how to live out their faith in a world in need of redemption. This exploration provides not only theological insight but also practical guidance for living in alignment with Christ's example and teachings.

CHAPTER 07

PRACTICAL IMPLICATIONS

How Understanding Jesus' Nature Affects Christian Faith and Practice

The dual nature of Jesus Christ—fully divine and fully human—and His sinlessness have profound implications for Christian faith and practice. This chapter explores how these fundamental truths influence everyday Christian living, worship, discipleship, and community life, helping believers to integrate their theological knowledge with practical expressions of faith.

Worship and Devotion

1. Object of Worship: Understanding Jesus as fully God justifies His place as the object of Christian worship. Worship practices, including prayer, singing hymns, and participating in sacraments like communion, are rooted in

recognizing His divinity and the sacrificial love displayed through His human experiences.

2. Depth of Devotion: Recognizing Jesus' sinlessness and His experiences of human temptation and suffering deepens the believer's emotional and spiritual connection to Him. It invites a more profound reverence and awe in worship, knowing that He overcame the world's trials yet understands them intimately.

Discipleship and Spiritual Growth

1. Moral and Ethical Modeling: Jesus' life provides a perfect model for behavior and ethics. Christians are called to emulate His actions and attitudes—His compassion, humility, zeal for justice, and obedience to God. This modeling affects decisions in personal, family, and professional life, guiding believers in conflict resolution, ethical dilemmas, and service.

2. Spiritual Disciplines: The human practices of Jesus, such as prayer, fasting, and scriptural meditation, serve as examples for believers. Understanding His commitment to these disciplines despite—or perhaps because of—His divine nature encourages believers to prioritize them in their spiritual growth.

Community and Relationships

1. Church Community: Jesus' example of fellowship and community, as seen in His interactions with His disciples

and followers, underscores the importance of church life. It encourages believers to invest in their local church communities, participate in small groups, and engage in communal worship and service projects.

2. Outreach and Evangelism: Jesus' command to love others and make disciples is empowered by His example and teachings. His approach to evangelism, characterized by both grace and truth, provides a template for how believers are to interact with the broader world, promoting the Gospel in a way that is both respectful and bold.

Social Justice and Service

1. Advocacy for the Marginalized: Jesus' ministry to the marginalized—such as the poor, the sick, and sinners—motivates Christians to engage in social justice and outreach activities. Understanding His nature and mission directs believers to areas of need and service, inspiring them to act as His hands and feet in the world.

2. Compassion and Empathy: Jesus' empathetic interactions, despite never sinning, allow believers to approach issues of injustice and suffering with a deep sense of compassion and empathy. This understanding influences how they respond to societal challenges, including poverty, inequality, and injustice.

Personal Identity and Vocation

1. Identity in Christ: Understanding Jesus' sinless human nature helps believers comprehend their new identity in Christ. This identity transcends cultural, social, and personal histories, grounding the believer's self-understanding of who Jesus is and what He has done.

2. Vocational Calling: Jesus' obedience to His divine calling, even to the point of death, provides a framework for understanding and pursuing one's vocation. Believers are encouraged to discern and live out their callings in alignment with God's will and purposes, as Jesus did.

Understanding the nature of Jesus—His divinity, humanity, and sinlessness—has far-reaching implications for how believers live out their faith. It shapes worship, influences moral behavior, molds community interactions, inspires social action, and defines personal and collective identity. This holistic impact fosters a faith that is not only believed in the heart and mind but also practiced in daily life, making the life of Jesus not only a historical fact to be revered but a living reality to be emulated.

APPLICATION OF JESUS' SINLESSNESS TO DAILY CHRISTIAN LIFE

Jesus' sinlessness is not merely a doctrinal cornerstone but also a practical guide for Christian living. This chapter explores how believers can apply the concept of Jesus' sinlessness to their daily lives, influencing their decisions, behaviors, and relationships, thereby reflecting Christ's character in the modern world.

Moral and Ethical Conduct

1. Personal Integrity: Jesus' sinlessness provides a perfect standard of moral integrity. Christians are encouraged to emulate His honesty, purity, and ethical behavior in all aspects of life, from personal relationships to business dealings. This involves avoiding deceit, corruption, and compromise, striving instead for transparency and fairness.

2. Conflict Resolution: In situations of conflict, Jesus' approach offers a model for resolution that prioritizes reconciliation and forgiveness over retaliation. His teachings on turning the other cheek and loving one's enemies (Matthew 5:38-48) challenge believers to handle disputes with grace and patience, aiming for peace rather than victory.

Spiritual Discipline

1. Prayer and Fasting: Jesus' commitment to prayer and fasting, even amidst His busy ministry, highlights the importance of these disciplines in maintaining spiritual strength and focus. Christians are encouraged to integrate regular prayer and fasting into their routines, seeking divine

guidance and strength to overcome temptations and challenges.

2. Scriptural Engagement: The way Jesus countered temptations by quoting Scripture underscores the power of God's Word in resisting sin. Believers are motivated to regularly read, study, and memorize the Bible, using it as their primary tool for understanding God's will and defending against moral and spiritual challenges.

Social Interaction and Community Engagement

1. Service and Humility: Jesus washed His disciples' feet, setting an example of service and humility (John 13:1-17). Christians are called to adopt a servant-leader model in both church settings and the broader community, seeking to serve rather than be served and elevating others' needs above their own.

2. Inclusive Relationships: Jesus' interactions with societal outcasts and sinners (Luke 19:1-10, John 4:1-26) demonstrate a radical inclusivity. Followers of Christ are encouraged to extend their community and social circles beyond comfortable boundaries, engaging with and loving those who are different from themselves.

Emotional and Mental Health

1. Handling Emotions: Jesus experienced a range of emotions, yet He managed them without sin. This teaches

believers to acknowledge their emotions—anger, sadness, joy—without letting these feelings lead to sinful actions. It also encourages seeking healthy emotional processing and expression.

2. Dependence on God: Jesus' prayer in Gethsemane (Matthew 26:36-46) reveals His dependence on the Father in times of extreme distress. This model encourages Christians to lean on God during their struggles, using prayer as a means to find peace and courage.

Worship and Devotional Life

1. Reverence in Worship: The sinlessness of Jesus enhances the reverence with which He is to be worshipped. Believers are reminded of His holiness and perfection, which inspires deeper awe and more sincere worship, whether in communal settings or in private devotion.

2. Ethical Consumption: Understanding that Jesus lived a life untainted by worldly corruption can lead Christians to consider the ethics of their consumption habits—how they spend their money, the products they buy, and the companies they support—striving to ensure that their resources do not contribute to exploitation or sin.

Applying the sinlessness of Jesus to daily Christian life transforms theoretical faith into practical action. Each aspect of life—moral, spiritual, social, emotional, and even economic—can be influenced profoundly by the example set by Christ. As believers strive to reflect Jesus' sinless nature in their own lives, they not only grow closer to Him but also become lights in the world, drawing others to the truth of the Gospel through their words and deeds. This chapter provides a roadmap for living out the implications of Christ's purity, offering a compelling vision of a life fully devoted to emulating the sinless Savior.

RECONCILING THEOLOGICAL TRUTHS WITH PERSONAL FAITH EXPERIENCES

Christian theology is rich with profound truths about God, humanity, and salvation. However, integrating these theological truths with personal faith experiences can sometimes be challenging. This chapter explores practical ways believers can reconcile deep theological doctrines, such as the sinlessness of Jesus, with their everyday faith experiences, enhancing their spiritual life and growth.

Understanding Theological Truths

1. Foundational Doctrines: Begin by outlining the core theological truths that need integration into personal faith, such as the Trinity, the incarnation of Jesus, His sinlessness, atonement, and resurrection. Understanding these doctrines

not only intellectually but also in their scriptural and historical contexts is crucial.

2. Theological Education: Encourage ongoing theological education through Bible studies, theological books, and courses. Education empowers believers to understand complex doctrines and see their relevance to personal and communal life.

Experiencing Faith Personally

1. Personal Prayer and Meditation: Engage in regular prayer and meditation on scriptural truths. This practice helps internalize theological concepts and transform them from abstract ideas into realities that impact daily living.

2. Spiritual Disciplines: Incorporate spiritual disciplines such as fasting, solitude, and contemplative reading into regular practice. These disciplines help deepen the connection between learned truths and personal spiritual encounters.

Bridging The Gap

1. Application in Life Challenges: Apply theological truths to real-life situations. For instance, understanding Jesus' response to suffering and temptation can offer practical ways to handle personal trials and temptations.

2. Testimonies and Storytelling: Share personal stories and testimonies within the community about how theological

truths have manifested in real life. This practice not only encourages others but also reinforces the personal relevance of these truths.

Community and Fellowship

1. Small Group Discussions: Participate in or form small groups focused on discussing and unpacking theological truths and their practical implications. These groups provide support and diverse perspectives that can enrich personal understanding and application.

2. Mentorship and Discipleship: Engage in mentorship or discipleship relationships. Learning from someone who embodies theological truths in their life can be incredibly impactful for personal spiritual growth.

Dealing with Doubts and Struggles

1. Open Dialogue: Foster an environment where doubts and struggles can be openly discussed without judgment. This approach can help reconcile head knowledge with heart faith, addressing areas where personal experiences seem to contradict theological understandings.

2. Theological Counseling: Utilize resources like pastoral counseling or Christian therapy when theological truths clash with personal experiences, especially during times of crisis, grief, or deep doubt.

Integration Through Worship

1. Liturgical Practices: Engage in worship practices that incorporate theological truths, such as communion, baptism, and liturgical readings. These practices can help internalize and celebrate these truths in a community setting.

2. Worship as Response: View worship not just as a duty but as a response to understanding God's nature and actions. This perspective helps personalize worship and align it more closely with personal beliefs and experiences.

Reconciling theological truths with personal faith experiences is essential for a vibrant and authentic Christian life. This process requires intentionality, education, community involvement, and personal reflection. By actively engaging with both theology and personal faith, believers can live out their beliefs more fully, making theology not just an academic study but a lived experience that informs guides, and enriches every aspect of life. This chapter aims to provide practical strategies and encouragement for those seeking to deepen their faith through a thoughtful integration of belief and experience.

THE SIGNIFICANCE OF JESUS" NATURE FOR CHRISTIAN BELIEF

Summary of Key Points Discussed

Throughout this exploration, we have delved into the complex and profound nature of Jesus Christ—His divinity, humanity, and sinlessness—and the significant impact these aspects have on Christian theology, practice, and personal faith. We have seen how the dual nature of Jesus as both fully God and fully human is foundational to Christian doctrine, offering a bridge between God and humanity that is unique and essential for salvation. His sinlessness, a critical aspect of His nature, not only qualifies Him as the perfect sacrifice for sin but also provides a moral and spiritual model for believers to emulate.

Final Thoughts on the Significance of Jesus' Nature for Christian Belief

The nature of Jesus Christ is not merely a theological assertion; it is the heartbeat of Christian faith. It informs our understanding of God's character—His holiness, love, and justice—and shapes our grasp of salvation, revealing a God who does not stand aloof from human suffering but enters into it to redeem us. Jesus' humanity assures us that God understands our weaknesses and struggles intimately, while His divinity guarantees that He has the power to save us completely.

The Role of Jesus' Sinlessness

Jesus' sinlessness is particularly compelling. It challenges us to reflect on the nature of sin and redemption. His life shows that it is possible to live in obedience to God's will, providing hope and a clear path for believers striving to overcome sin. Moreover, Jesus' sinlessness in the face of temptation provides a trustworthy foundation for His role as our mediator and advocate before God.

Ongoing Relevance of Understanding Jesus' Humanity, Divinity, and Sinlessness

In a world rife with moral ambiguity and spiritual confusion, the clear example and teaching of Jesus Christ stand as a beacon of truth and authority. Understanding Jesus' humanity allows believers to feel deeply connected to Him—encouraged that He knows our pains and joys. His divinity offers a constant reminder of His supreme authority and the transformative power available to us through faith. Meanwhile, His sinlessness serves as both a challenge to personal holiness and a comfort that our salvation is secure, not by our efforts but by His perfect sacrifice.

The ongoing relevance of these truths cannot be overstated. In every generation, the church must reclaim and rearticulate the significance of Jesus' life and work to remain faithful to the gospel and effective in its mission. As society changes, the timeless truths of Jesus' nature continue to provide wisdom, guidance and hope for all who seek to follow Him.

Closing Remarks

As we conclude this exploration, let each reader be inspired to delve deeper into the mystery and majesty of Jesus Christ. May our study not only enrich our minds but transform our hearts and lives, leading us to worship with greater awe, live with greater faithfulness, and share His love with greater fervor. In understanding more fully who Jesus is, we find the foundation for all aspects of Christian life—from the personal journey of faith to the communal pursuit of God's kingdom on earth. Let us, therefore, hold fast to these truths, allowing them to guide us in all we do, for the glory of God and the advancement of His gospel in the world.

APPENDIX

ADDITIONAL RESOURCES

Recommended Readings for Further Study

Understanding the nature and significance of Jesus Christ is an ongoing journey that can be enriched by engaging with a range of theological works. Below is a list of recommended readings that provide deeper insights into His divinity, humanity, and sinlessness, as well as the broader implications for Christian theology and practice:

1. "Mere Christianity" by C.S. Lewis - This classic work provides a clear and accessible explanation of Christian beliefs, including the nature of Jesus.

2. "The Case for Christ" by Lee Strobel - A journalistic exploration of the evidence for Jesus' life, death, and resurrection.

3. "Jesus of Nazareth" by Pope Benedict XVI - This detailed examination by a theological scholar offers deep insights into the historical Jesus and His teachings.

4. "Knowing Christ" by Mark Jones - This book delves into the person and work of Christ, emphasizing His attributes and their relevance for believers.

5. "The Person of Christ" by Donald Macleod - A comprehensive doctrinal study focusing on the nature of Christ, including a thorough discussion of the hypostatic union.

6. "Christology in the Making" by James D.G. Dunn - A New Testament scholar provides a historical examination of how early Christians understood Jesus.

7. "The Cross of Christ" by John Stott - This work explores the achievements of Christ as a result of His crucifixion, particularly focusing on the theological implications of His atonement and sacrifice.

8. "Orthodoxy" by G.K. Chesterton - A spirited defense of Christianity that includes poignant reflections on Christ's paradoxical qualities as both God and man.

9. "The Resurrection of the Son of God" by N.T. Wright - An in-depth look at the historical and theological significance of the resurrection of Jesus.

10. "Desiring God" by John Piper - Although not exclusively about Christology, this book presents a vision of Christian life and faith that is Christ-centered and deeply rooted in Scripture.

Glossary of Theological Terms

To aid in understanding the discussions throughout this book, here is a glossary of key theological terms related to the study of Jesus Christ:

- Atonement: The reconciliation between God and humanity brought about through the life, death, and resurrection of Jesus.

- Christology: The branch of Christian theology relating to the nature, person, and works of Jesus Christ.

- Divinity: The nature of being God; in Christian theology, this refers to Jesus' godly nature as part of the Trinity.

- Hypostatic Union: The doctrine that Jesus Christ is one Person in two natures, fully divine and fully human.

- Impeccability: The doctrine that Christ could not sin.

- Incarnation: The belief that God became flesh in the person of Jesus Christ.

- Mediator: One who intervenes between two parties, especially for the purpose of reconciling differences; Jesus is seen as the mediator between God and humanity.

- Propitiation: A sacrifice that bears God's wrath to the end and in so doing changes God's wrath toward man into favor.

- Soteriology: The study of religious doctrines of salvation. In Christianity, this is focused on the roles of Jesus in the salvation of humanity.

- Trinity: The Christian doctrine that God exists as three persons but is one being.

This appendix is designed to complement the theological exploration in the main text, offering additional resources for those who wish to deepen their understanding and apply their faith more profoundly in their daily lives.

www.ingramcontent.com/pod-product-compliance
Lightning Source LLC
Chambersburg PA
CBHW061321120726
48001CB00002B/627